W9-DBO-805

TABLE OF CONTENTS

CHAPTER 1

THE MIRACLE METS

The last batted ball of the 1969 World Series was a deep fly hit by the Baltimore Orioles' Davey Johnson. New York Mets left fielder Cleon Jones settled beneath it at the edge of the Shea Stadium warning track. He said to himself, "Come down, baby. Come down, baby." When it did, he squeezed the baseball into his glove and dropped to one knee.

As Jones sank to the occasion, fans began to swarm onto the field to celebrate. The impossible dream had become reality. Baseball's lovable losers had become world champions.

Only a hopeless optimist would have predicted the Mets would become baseball's best team that year. In their seven previous seasons, they had averaged 56 wins and 105 losses and had never finished higher than ninth place in the 10-team National League (NL).

Pitcher Jerry Koosman jumps into the arms of catcher Jerry Grote on October 16, 1969, after the Mets won their first World Series.

A STRONG LEADER

Gil Hodges hit 370 major league home runs, including the first in Mets history.

But the team's fans remember him most for being the no-nonsense manager who turned the ballclub into a winner. Hired in October 1967, he instilled discipline and confidence in the players. In May 1969, with the team struggling, he gave a clubhouse speech. "He chewed us out, but he didn't embarrass anybody," second baseman Ken Boswell said. "We aren't playing up to our potential. He knows we can."

Soon the Mets were winning, in part because of a platoon system under which Hodges played left-handed hitters against right-handed pitchers and righty hitters against lefty pitchers at first base, second base, third base, and right field.

In April 1972, Mets players and fans were left with heavy hearts when their leader died of a heart attack at age 47.

Catcher Jerry Grote was one of the first believers. He told some teammates in spring training that they could "win it all." Pitching star Tom Seaver thought Grote was crazy. "My eyes started to roll," Seaver said, "and I looked at him like he was nuts."

Grote did not look very smart when New York dropped five straight games to fall to 18–23. The Mets were nine games out in the new six-team NL East. But that is when the team parted with its sorry history. New York won its next 11 games, including one in 15 innings. The Mets moved into second place behind the Chicago Cubs.

On July 8, the Cubs came to Shea leading the division by 5 1/2 games. That afternoon, the Mets had just one hit entering the ninth inning. However, they scored three

Tom Seaver delivers a pitch for the Mets in 1969. Seaver finished the season 25–7 with a 2.21 ERA and won the NL's Cy Young Award.

runs to rally for a 4–3 victory. The next night was even more exciting. The Mets won 4–0. Seaver retired the first 25 Cubs before a single by Jimmy Qualls spoiled his bid for a perfect game. Less than two weeks later, the nation was mesmerized by Apollo 11. "When the astronauts walked on the moon, I figured we had a chance to win," reliever Tug McGraw said. "Nothing seemed impossible after that."

Instead of reaching baseball's stratosphere, however, New York took a giant leap backward. The Mets plummeted to

Mets center fielder Tommie Agee prepares to make a diving catch in Game 3 of the 1969 World Series.

third place and 10 games behind on August 13. That is when the Mets became miraculous. They won 12 of their next 13 games and 38 of their final 49. New York moved into first place on September 10 and clinched the division on September 24. The Mets finished 100–62, eight games in front of the Cubs.

The best was yet to come. To reach the World Series, the Mets, a team built on pitching and defense, would have to beat the NL West champion Atlanta Braves and Hall of Fame slugger Hank Aaron in a best-of-five series. The Mets could not stop Aaron, who homered three times. But the Braves could not stop the Mets. New York won 9–5, 11–6, and 7–4 to capture the pennant in a three-game sweep in the NL Championship Series (NLCS).

Now, all that stood between the Mets and a world championship were the Baltimore Orioles. The Orioles won 109 games in the regular season. This was more than any American League (AL) team since 1961. Don Buford, Baltimore's first batter in Game 1 of the World Series, homered off Seaver. The host Orioles won the opener 4–1. It appeared the Mets had finally met their match.

But Jerry Koosman was brilliant in the second game. He pitched no-hit ball for six innings. After Baltimore tied the score at 1–1 in the bottom of the seventh, the Mets used ninth-inning singles by Ed Charles, Grote, and Al Weis to provide the winning 2–1 margin.

Suddenly, the Series was tied at one win apiece and heading back to New York. Tommie Agee led off the bottom of the first inning of Game 3 with a home run. But his biggest heroics came on defense. With two men out in the fourth inning and two Orioles on base, the center fielder made a sprinting backhanded catch of a drive to the left-center-field wall hit by Elrod Hendricks. In the seventh, the Orioles had the bases loaded with two outs when

The Mighty Met

Infielder Al Weis, who weighed all of 160 pounds, hit just .219 with seven home runs in 800 career regular-season games. But in Game 2 of the 1969 World Series, he singled in Ed Charles with the winning run in the ninth inning. And in Game 5, he tied the score at 3–3 with a home run off Dave McNally. Weis batted .455 for the Series.

Agee robbed Paul Blair with a diving grab in right-center. The sensational plays had cost the Orioles five runs in a 5–0 Mets victory.

The Mets used more defensive wizardry to prevail in Game 4. With New York leading 1–0 in the ninth and two Orioles on base, Brooks Robinson lined a pitch to right field. Ron Swoboda raced to his right and dived headlong. If the ball had eluded him, both runners would have scored. But the outfielder made a spectacular catch. A run came in from third base on the play. But the Orioles' rally was cut short. And in the 10th

inning, the Mets scored the winning run on a bad throw. They moved to within one win of the championship.

The Orioles took a 3–0 lead in Game 5. But the Mets clawed back. They scored twice in the sixth inning on a home run by first baseman Donn Clendenon, the World Series Most Valuable Player (MVP). New York then tied the score in the seventh on a homer by Weis. In the eighth, Swoboda doubled in Jones and a second run scored on a misplayed grounder. All that was left was for Koosman to retire the Orioles in the ninth. He did, with the final out landing in Jones's glove.

Fans streamed onto the field to celebrate, and the team poured into its clubhouse. There, Casey Stengel, the Mets' first manager, congratulated manager Gil Hodges. Stengel stopped to consider the

He Said It

"Long live democracy, free speech, and the '69 Mets—all improbable, glorious miracles that I have always believed in."

—Movie actor and baseball fan Tim Robbins

Fans celebrate in the stands at Shea Stadium as the Mets rejoice after winning the 1969 World Series in five games over the Orioles.

Mets' sudden climb from their humble beginnings just seven seasons earlier when they finished 40–120. "They came slow," Stengel said, "but fast."

Four days later, the team was given a ticker-tape parade in Manhattan, just as the Apollo 11 astronauts were two months earlier. Said catcher J. C. Martin, "We might as well have walked on the moon ourselves."

CHAPTER 2

MEET THE METS

T he Mets' theme song, "Meet the Mets," was released in 1963. This was during the team's second season. The song hints at the fans' special relationship with the team. It talks about "the butcher and the baker and the people on the streets . . . hollerin' and cheerin' and jumpin' in their seats."

If the Yankees had become New York's team of champions, the Mets would become the team that championed its fans.

The Mets had their origins in the city's love of NL baseball. The Brooklyn Dodgers and the New York Giants had played in New York since the late 1800s.

But after the 1957 season, both NL teams left for California. Supporters of the teams were heartbroken. Most did not want to root for the AL Yankees. They had long considered them the enemy. So, Mayor Robert Wagner appointed a panel to find a replacement team.

Veteran first baseman Gil Hodges, shown in January 1962, holds the contract he signed with the Mets before the team's first season.

The Name Game

Fans helped select the team's name by voting in a newspaper poll. The choices were Continentals, Sky-liners, Mets, Jets, Meadowlarks, Burros, Skyscrapers, Rebels, NYBs, and Avengers. The runner-up was Skyliners. Club owner Joan Payson preferred Meadowlarks. Mets is tied to the organization's corporate name, the Metropolitan Baseball Club Inc., and recalls an 1880s New York team: the Metropolitans.

One of the group's leaders, William Shea, tried to get the Philadelphia Phillies, the Cincinnati Reds, and the Pittsburgh Pirates to move to town. But they would not leave their homes. Then, he tried to persuade the NL to expand. But its leaders did not want to. Finally, he and some other business executives formed the new Continental League in 1959. The league was scheduled to begin play in 1961. NL owners feared having to compete with a new league for fans. As a result, they changed their minds and granted expansion teams to Houston, in late 1960, and New York, in early 1961. And so the Mets were born.

The ballclub adopted the Dodgers' blue and the Giants' orange and announced that its manager would be Casey Stengel. Stengel had played for both teams and managed the Dodgers and the Yankees. The team would play at the Polo Grounds, the former Manhattan home of the Giants. In the expansion draft, the Mets selected former Dodgers Gil Hodges, Don Zimmer, and Roger Craig. On a Thanksgiving Day parade float, the 71-year-old Stengel said his new team was going to be "terrific, wonderful, amazin'."

It turned out the Mets were amazingly bad. In its first regular-season game, New York lost 11–4 to the visiting

Mets manager Casey Stengel, *left*, shakes hands with Pirates manager Danny Murtaugh before New York's first home game ever in April 1962.

St. Louis Cardinals. The Mets gave up 16 hits, allowed three stolen bases, and committed three errors. They dropped their next eight games, too. Then, it got worse. The season included losing streaks of 11, 13, and 17 games.

Perhaps the most hapless Met had the initials M. E. T.: Marvin Eugene Throneberry.

True Colors

The circular Mets logo, designed by Ray Gatto, was introduced in 1961. The bridge shows that New York's five boroughs are linked. The skyline reflects many of the city's skyscrapers, including the Empire State Building and United Nations. Blue and orange are the state colors and were used by the 1964 World's Fair, which was held next to Shea Stadium.

First baseman Marv Throneberry poses in 1962. Throneberry's comical failures made him fit right in on a terrible Mets team.

The power-hitting first base-man's exploits made him a fan favorite. His butter-fingered failures made him even more beloved. On June 17, in a typical game for "Marvelous Marv," he was called for defensive interference in the top of the first inning. This allowed a base runner to score. In the bottom half, Throneberry hit what appeared to be a triple. But he was ruled out on an appeal play because he failed to touch first base. Stengel came out of the dugout to argue. But coach Cookie Lavagetto intercepted him and said, "Forget it, Casey. He missed second, too."

When the club celebrated Stengel's birthday in July, Throneberry complained he had not gotten his piece of cake. Said Stengel, "We were going to give you a piece, Marv. But we were afraid you'd drop it."

Throneberry was not the only Met to bumble defensively. Early in the season, center fielder Richie Ashburn and shortstop Elio Chacon collided while chasing a fly ball. Chacon did not speak English, so Ashburn learned to say, "Yo la tengo," which is Spanish for "I got it." Later in the season, Ashburn called, "Yo la tengo," when a fly was hit to short left-center and was pleased to see Chacon backing off. Ashburn got ready to make the catch and instead was bowled over by left fielder Frank Thomas, who did not understand Spanish.

The losing frustrated Stengel, who had won seven World Series as Yankees manager. Often during the 1962 season, he would complain, "Can't anybody here play this game?"

Not the Mets. They finished 60 games out of first place with a record of 40–120. They had more losses than any team since 1899.

They lost 120 games but won the hearts of nearly a million people. Their attendance of 922,530 was at the time the second best in baseball history

The Sign Man

Karl Ehrhardt gave voice to Mets fans with his use of the written word. A commercial artist, he attended games at Shea Stadium from 1964 to 1981 with a folder filled with 30 to 40 oversized signs that he displayed to comment on the action. From his field-level seat behind third base, he would hold up "WHAT FOOLS WE METS FANS BE" or "BACK TO YOUR NEST, BIRD!" or his famous message when the Mets won the 1969 World Series: "THERE ARE NO WORDS."

"TOM TERRIFIC"

Like magic, the best player in Mets history was pulled out of a hat.

After the Atlanta Braves broke a baseball rule by signing Tom Seaver after his 1966 college season had started, major league commissioner William D. Eckert put the names of other teams interested in signing the pitcher into a hat. The slip of paper saying "Mets" was selected.

Seaver won the NL Rookie of the Year Award in 1967, and two years later he received the first of his three Cy Young Awards as the best pitcher in the league. He also was the NL Cy Young winner in 1973 and 1975. Seaver pitched for the Mets through mid-1977 and returned for the 1983 season.

Seaver won 311 career games, 198 of them with the Mets. He was elected to the Hall of Fame in 1992 with his name selected on 98.84 percent of the ballots, the highest percentage in history.

for a last-place team. The fans were loud and enthusiastic. They laughed to keep from crying. They chanted, "Let's Go, Mets!" and hung bedsheets with messages supporting the team.

The Mets kept losing games: 111 in 1963, 109 in 1964, and 112 in 1965. But attendance soared, and the team's younger players, called "The Youth of America" by Stengel, began to make a positive impact. Outfielder Jim Hickman was the first Met to hit three homers in a game and the first to hit for the cycle (a single, double, triple, and homer in the same game). Second-year second baseman Ron Hunt became an All-Star starter in 1964. First baseman Ed Kranepool was a 20-year-old All-Star in 1965. In the minor leagues, the Mets began developing

The interior of Shea Stadium, including its large scoreboard in right field, is shown during a night game in 1964. The Mets' ballpark opened that year.

players such as Cleon Jones, Bud Harrelson, Jerry Koosman, and Nolan Ryan.

Soon the youngsters had a new playpen: Shea Stadium in Queens. The tall, circular ballpark opened in 1964 and drew 1,732,597 fans. This was the second most in the majors and 426,959 more than the Yankees, who won their fifth straight AL pennant that year. The Mets finished in last place, of course. But fans were treated to escalator rides, the major leagues' largest scoreboard, and a new live mascot: Mr. Met.

In several years, they would be treated to a miracle, too.

CHAPTER 3

YA GOTTA BELIEVE

By the afternoon of July 9, 1973, the Mets were no longer miraculous. The team had finished in third place in 1970, 1971, and 1972. Now, it had slipped into last place at 34–46 and 12 1/2 games behind in the NL East.

No one was more frustrated than Tug McGraw, an energetic left-hander who celebrated victories by slapping his thigh with his glove. Praised by Cincinnati Reds manager Sparky Anderson after the 1972 season as the "Seaver of saves," the relief pitcher was struggling that season. But he was determined to turn things around—for himself and the team.

Earlier that day, McGraw visited friend Joe Badamo, who told him, "You've got to believe in yourself." Driving to Shea Stadium, McGraw kept repeating the phrase in his mind. When fans outside the ballpark asked him what was wrong

Relief pitcher Tug McGraw, the inspirational leader of the 1973 Mets, gives a thumbs-up sign after the team won Game 5 of the World Series.

"SHEA HEY KID"

Mets team owner Joan Payson's favorite player was center fielder Willie Mays, who became a superstar with the New York Giants before the team moved to San Francisco for the 1958 season.

For years, Payson wanted to bring Mays back to New York. She finally succeeded in May 1972, when the Mets acquired Mays from the Giants for pitcher Charlie Williams and $50,000.

Mays, then 41, drove in the winning run with a home run in his first game as a Met, a 5-4 home triumph over his former team. The victory was part of an 11-game winning streak that led *Sports Illustrated* magazine to put Mays on the cover and call New York "The Amaysing Mets."

Mays's last hit was a single that drove in the winning run in Game 2 of the 1973 World Series. He hit 660 career homers and was elected to the Hall of Fame on the first ballot.

with the team, he answered, "Nothing! Ya gotta believe!"

That afternoon, Mets board chairman M. Donald Grant gave a clubhouse pep talk. He told the players that management remained confident in their chances. McGraw got up from his stool and hollered, "He's right! He's right! Just believe. Ya gotta believe!" His words became a team rallying cry.

Manager Yogi Berra also told players to keep the faith. He kept saying, "It ain't over 'til it's over."

By August 30, the inspired Mets were still in last place at 61–71. But they had cut their deficit to 6 1/2 games. Then, New York won 21 of its final 29 games. Many of the wins were thrilling. On September 18, the Mets scored five runs in the top of the ninth to defeat Pittsburgh 6–5. Two nights

Willie Mays, in a suit because he was on the disabled list, talks with Mets teammates, *from left*, Jim Fregosi, Jon Matlack, and Rusty Staub in May 1973.

later, this time in New York, they prevailed 4–3 after a Pirates runner was thrown out at the plate in the 13th on a ball that hit the top edge of the left-field fence.

The Mets clinched the division on October 1 with a 6–4 victory over the Cubs in Chicago that made their final record 82–79. McGraw, who recorded the last nine outs, was brilliant in the season's closing two months. He won five games and saved 14 more.

In the Wrigley Field club-house, he jumped onto an equipment trunk and kept yelling, "Ya gotta believe." His teammates hollered the same

Mets manager Yogi Berra, *middle*, speaks with pitchers Tom Seaver, *left*, and Jon Matlack during a workout in preparation for the 1973 NLCS.

"Le Grand Orange"

Daniel Joseph Staub received his nicknames "Rusty" and "Le Grand Orange" (French for "The Big Orange") because of his red hair. Acquired from the Montreal Expos in 1972, the right fielder was a key contributor for the Mets in the 1973 postseason. He hit three homers in the NLCS and collected 11 hits and six runs batted in (RBIs) in the World Series despite playing with an injured right shoulder.

phrase back, just as enthusiastically. Next up was a best-of-five NLCS against the favored Cincinnati Reds. After dropping the opener, visiting New York evened the series on a 5–0 two-hitter by Jon Matlack. The Mets won 9–2 at Shea in a Game 3 that was marred by a fight between shortstop Bud Harrelson and hard-sliding

Reds base runner Pete Rose. A 12th-inning homer by Rose gave Game 4 to Cincinnati. But New York took the pennant with a 7–2 victory in Game 5. Again, McGraw was on the mound at the end.

The underdog Mets faced the powerful Oakland Athletics in the World Series and nearly prevailed. They won 10–7 on the road in Game 2 with four runs in the 12th inning; 6–1 in Game 4 at Shea on a five-hitter by Matlack and Ray Sadecki; and 2–0 in Game 5 at home on a three-hitter by Jerry Koosman and McGraw. But the magic ran out in the final two games in Oakland. "I was believing," McGraw said, "right up to the last out."

The Mets' run was over. The team sank to fifth place in 1974 and finished fifth or last every season from 1977 through 1983. But in 1984,

Hometown Kid

The Mets selected Lee Mazzilli, who was raised in Brooklyn, in the first round of the 1973 amateur draft. The center fielder broke into the big leagues with the Mets in late 1976 and quickly became a fan favorite. In the 1979 All-Star Game, "The Italian Stallion" homered to tie the score in the eighth inning, then walked with the bases loaded in the ninth for a 7-6 NL victory. He was traded in 1982, then returned to the Mets in 1986 and was a clutch pinch-hitter that postseason.

Davey Johnson, who had made the last out of the 1969 World Series, became the Mets' new manager. And the team's fortunes would soar again.

CHAPTER 4

EXTRA-INNING MAGIC

T he message that briefly and accidentally flashed on the Shea Stadium scoreboard on October 25, 1986, seemed to say it all: "Congratulations, Boston Red Sox, World Champions."

There was no joy in Metville. New York trailed the World Series three games to two and was behind 5–3 in Game 6 with nobody on base and two out in the 10th inning. Star first baseman Keith Hernandez was so disappointed after making the second out that he had already left the dugout for the clubhouse. Utility player

The Big Apple

In 1980, Shea Stadium debuted a 9-foot-wide fiberboard apple beyond the center-field fence. The oversized piece of red fruit rose from an upside-down plywood top hat and lit up whenever a Met hit a home run. The apple, which was part of an advertising campaign called "The Magic Is Back," is now displayed outside the Jackie Robinson Rotunda at Citi Field. A newer, shinier apple now celebrates Mets homers.

Ray Knight is greeted by Mets teammate Howard Johnson as he scores the winning run in Game 6 of the 1986 World Series. New York rallied for three runs with two outs to beat Boston 6–5 in 10 innings.

Kevin Mitchell was on the phone making plane reservations home to California. NBC officials were hanging plastic sheets over the Red Sox's lockers to protect the players' belongings from champagne spray. All hope appeared lost for the Mets.

But, as Yogi Berra said 13 years earlier, "It ain't over 'til it's over." The confident Mets would not go quietly into the

From Throneberry to Strawberry

Marv Throneberry was the Mets' first left-handed power hitter. But Darryl Strawberry, who also hit left-handed, was their best power hitter ever. The sweet-swinging right fielder was named Rookie of the Year in 1983 and reached 200 homers sooner than any other major leaguer to that point (at age 27 in 1989). Through 2013, he held the Mets record for home runs with 252. But his career was shortened by substance abuse, injuries, and illness.

New York night. They were able to draw strength from a regular season filled with success and from an NLCS that tested their will.

In spring training, manager Davey Johnson had said, "We don't want to just win. We want to dominate." And the Mets did. New York won 20 of its first 24 games and took the NL East by 21 1/2 games with a club-record 108 victories. The offense led the league in runs. The pitching staff ranked first in earned-run average (ERA).

In the NLCS against the Houston Astros, the Mets proved their backbone. They won Game 2 at the Astrodome by beating Hall of Famer Nolan Ryan 5–1, then took the third game 6–5 on a two-run ninth-inning homer at Shea by center fielder Lenny Dykstra.

New York went up three games to two in the series when

Darryl Strawberry watches his solo home run in the fifth inning of the Mets' 2–1, 12-inning victory over the Astros in Game 5 of the 1986 NLCS.

catcher Gary Carter hit an RBI single in the bottom of the 12th in Game 5. It was the longest game in NL playoff history— until one day later. Game 6 in the Astrodome was one of the most thrilling in baseball history. The Mets wanted badly to

end the series so they would not have to play a Game 7 against Astros ace Mike Scott. Scott had shut down the Mets 1–0 in Game 1 and 3–1 in Game 4. But New York's bats were silent in Game 6. The Mets managed only two hits through eight innings

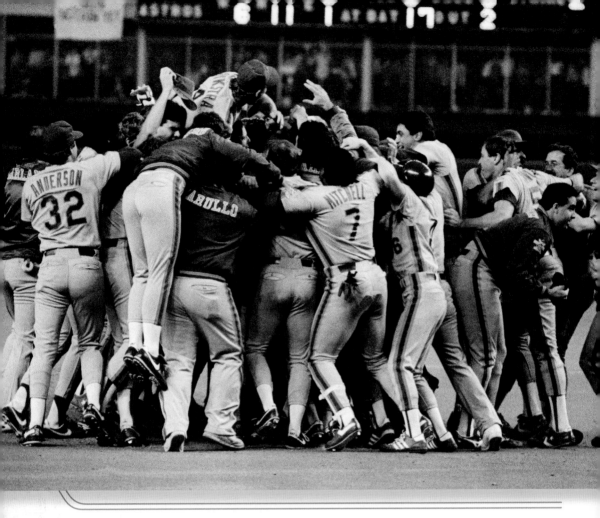

The Mets celebrate after clinching the pennant with a 7–6, 16-inning victory over the Astros in Game 6 of the 1986 NLCS.

off left-hander Bob Knepper. Then pinch-hitter Dykstra led off the ninth with a triple to center and scored on a single by center fielder Mookie Wilson. After a ground-out, Hernandez doubled home Wilson. Three batters later, third baseman Ray Knight hit a sacrifice fly and the score was tied.

"All I could think about was, 'We have a new life.' And this was the character of that ballclub," Carter said.

The Mets went ahead 4–3 in the 14th inning on an RBI single by second baseman Wally Backman. But the Astros' Billy Hatcher tied the game with a homer to left off Mets closer Jesse Orosco. The Mets responded by scoring three times in the 16th on RBI singles by Knight and Dykstra and on a wild pitch. Orosco then was able to shut the door. Barely. He allowed two runs in the bottom of the inning, then struck out Kevin Bass swinging with two men on to end it.

Orosco flung his glove into the air, and the exhausted Mets celebrated their pennant. Said Wilson, "It was a classic. I don't think anything that happens in the World Series can top it." Little did he know.

The Mets dug themselves a big hole by losing the first two games of the World Series at home. They won the next

"DR. K"

Dwight "Doc" Gooden had one of the best starts to a career in baseball history. At 19 years old in 1984, he became the youngest player to be named Rookie of the Year and play in an All-Star Game. As the season progressed, fans at Shea began celebrating each of his strikeouts by hanging a sign with the letter "K" near the left-field foul pole. He led the majors with 276 strikeouts.

The next year, Gooden went 24–4 with a 1.53 ERA, becoming the youngest Cy Young Award winner and youngest 20-game winner. He led the big leagues in strikeouts again, with 268. And in 1986, he was 17–6 in helping the Mets to the world championship.

Injury problems and drug abuse cost Gooden the chance to make the Hall of Fame. He pitched for the Mets through 1994 and finished his career with 194 victories and 112 losses. He pitched a no-hitter for the New York Yankees in 1996.

two at Fenway Park. But they then dropped Game 5, also in Boston. To win the Series, New York would have to win the final two games at Shea.

Game 6 was a tense affair, much like Game 6 in the NLCS. The Mets tied the score in the eighth inning on a sacrifice fly by Carter. But Boston's Dave Henderson silenced the crowd by homering off reliever Rick Aguilera in the 10th. Marty Barrett singled home an insurance run.

The Mets were down to their last three outs, then two outs, then one. But Carter singled to left, Mitchell returned from the clubhouse to single to center, and Knight blooped a two-strike single to center. Suddenly, the Mets were down by only a run with runners at first and third. Shea was rocking. Bob Stanley relieved Calvin Schiraldi and threw a wild pitch to Wilson that enabled Mitchell to score the tying run and Knight to reach second. And when Wilson tapped a grounder to first base that rolled under Bill Buckner's mitt, Knight skipped home with the winning run.

"It was like I was on a carpet," Knight recalled. "I was just floating home."

The Mets had to rally in Game 7, too. Boston scored three runs in the second inning before New York tied it with three in the sixth. Knight put the Mets ahead with a homer in the seventh off Schiraldi, and New York entered the ninth up 8–5.

Orosco was called on to protect the lead, as he did against the Astros. And again, the left-hander recorded the final out with a strikeout. He hurled his glove skyward, dropped to his knees, and raised his fists.

Mets players celebrated with a dog pile near the mound.

Ray Knight follows the flight of his go-ahead solo homer during the seventh inning of the Mets' 8–5 victory in Game 7 of the 1986 World Series.

Said Carter, "We hugged, jumped on each other, wrestled, fell down, got up, and laughed 'til we wept."

The franchise had its second championship and seemed poised for many more. As of 2013, Mets fans were still waiting.

CHAPTER 5

IN SEARCH OF MORE GLORY

The Mets slumped in 1987 but returned to form in 1988. They won the NL East by 15 games with a 100–60 record. Right fielder Darryl Strawberry hit 39 home runs. Right-hander David Cone went 20–3. Again, a balanced New York team led the league in runs scored and ERA.

In the NLCS, the Mets faced the Los Angeles Dodgers, a team they had beaten 10 of 11 times during the regular season. But they ran into a hot pitcher, Orel Hershiser. He allowed just three earned runs in 24 2/3 postseason innings, including a 6–0 shutout to win Game 7 in Los Angeles.

"After the game, I sat down in front of my locker and cried like a baby," Strawberry said.

What could have been a 1980s dynasty had resulted in just two playoff berths and five close calls: second-place finishes in 1984, 1985, 1987, 1989, and 1990. The Mets would bottom out in 1993 at 59–103.

Mets catcher Gary Carter shows the ball to the umpire, but Dodgers pitcher Brian Holton, *right*, was called safe at home in Game 6 of the 198 NLCS. New York won the game 5–1 but lost the series in seven games.

Late in the 1996 season, Bobby Valentine took over as manager. He brought a new energy to the team. The Mets won 88 games in 1997, then made two key trades early in 1998 with the Florida Marlins, acquiring power-hitting catcher Mike Piazza and starting pitcher Al Leiter. New York won another 88 games in 1998 but lost its final five and missed the playoffs by just a game.

Grand-Slam Single

The Mets faced elimination in Game 5 of the 1999 NLCS and trailed the Atlanta Braves by a run in the bottom of the 15th inning when backup catcher Todd Pratt walked with the bases loaded to force in the tying run. The next batter, third baseman Robin Ventura, sent a drive over the right-field fence to win the game. Mets players were so happy that they tackled Ventura between first and second, and he never got to round the bases. So, instead of a grand slam, he was credited with a long single.

In 1999, the Mets returned to the postseason, but just barely. Another late-season slump—seven straight losses from September 21 to September 28—nearly dashed their hopes. But they won their last three regular-season games, then faced the Cincinnati Reds in a one-game playoff for the wild card. Leiter came through with a two-hit shutout in Cincinnati as New York won 5–0.

The Mets faced the Arizona Diamondbacks in the NL Division Series (NLDS). The Mets won two of the first three games, then went to the bottom of the 10th inning of Game 4 tied at 3–3. New York backup catcher Todd Pratt lifted a fly ball to center field. Steve Finley drifted to the fence, leaped, and thought he caught the baseball. But when he came down, his glove was empty and the umpire was twirling his finger, signaling a home run.

Todd Pratt (7) celebrates his series-clinching homer in the Mets' 4–3, 10-inning victory over the Diamondbacks in Game 4 of the 1999 NLDS.

The walk-off shot propelled the Mets to the NLCS against the Atlanta Braves. New York lost the first three games but rallied to win the fourth game. The Mets came back from a run down in the 15th to take Game 5 at home, then fell behind 5–0 in Game 6 in Atlanta. They rallied but were eliminated 10–9 on a bases-loaded walk in the 11th inning.

"We gave everything we had," Valentine said. "There's not a lot left out on that field."

Mets manager Bobby Valentine, *middle*, removes pitcher Al Leiter, *right*, from Game 5 of the 2000 World Series. Catcher Mike Piazza is at left.

In 2000, the Mets returned to the playoffs as a wild card. They lost the first game of the NLDS in San Francisco, then beat the Giants in Game 2 on a 10th-inning single by center fielder Jay Payton. New York won Game 3 on a walk-off homer by left fielder Benny Agbayani in the 13th and clinched the series with a Game 4 one-hitter by right-hander Bobby Jones. This time, the Mets cruised in the NLCS. They beat the St. Louis Cardinals four games to one, winning the clincher at home on a three-hitter by left-hander Mike Hampton.

The victory set up a World Series matchup with the cross-town Yankees. New York City was aglow with anticipation. The Empire State Building was lit half in Mets colors and half in Yankees colors. Team logos were painted on train cars for what came to be known as the "Subway Series." But the Mets never got on track, losing in five games. Three of the defeats were by one run, then Game 5 was lost when the Yankees broke a 2–2 tie in the top of the ninth on Luis Sojo's single. The hit to center field drove in Jorge Posada. As Posada was sliding into home, the throw from Payton hit him and bounced into the Yankees' dugout. This allowed another run to score. The Yankees won 4–2 and took the Series.

"WE'RE ALL NEW YORKERS"

After terrorists destroyed the World Trade Center in New York on September 11, 2001, baseball games were canceled for a week to help the city and the nation mourn and heal.

Games in New York were not played until September 21, when the Mets hosted the Atlanta Braves. Players wore caps from local police and fire departments to honor their relief efforts. The Mets trailed by a run in the eighth inning with a man on base when catcher Mike Piazza crushed the ball over the center-field fence for the eventual 3–2 margin of victory.

Through 2013, Piazza had more homers than any other catcher in major league history. But none was more important than this one. "I'm glad to give people a diversion from the sorrow, to give them a thrill," he said. "If this helps, we're all New Yorkers."

Through 2013, the Mets had not been back to the Series since. They came close in 2006. That year, New York won 97 games behind a powerful offense led by center fielder Carlos Beltran, first baseman Carlos Delgado, third baseman David Wright, and shortstop Jose Reyes. The Mets swept the Dodgers in the NLDS but lost Game 7 of the NLCS at home to the Cardinals on a ninth-inning homer by Yadier Molina.

The Catch

With Game 7 of the 2006 NLCS tied at 1–1 in the sixth inning at Shea, the Cardinals' Scott Rolen drove a pitch into the St. Louis bullpen. Or so it seemed. Reserve left fielder Endy Chavez raced back and reached far over the fence to snare the ball in the tip of his glove. Then he fired toward the infield, where a Cardinals runner was doubled off first base. The Mets lost the game, but the catch is regarded by many baseball followers as one of the best in playoff history.

One season later, the Mets appeared ready to return to the postseason but blew a seven-game lead with 17 to play. "We played beyond horrible," Wright said. "We just gradually let this thing get away." The Mets stumbled down the stretch again in 2008. They failed to hold an advantage of 3 1/2 games with 17 remaining despite late-season heroics from ace left-hander Johan Santana.

The Mets drew a club-record 4,042,045 fans that season and said good-bye to their ballpark as Tom Seaver threw out the ceremonial last pitch to Piazza. The team moved in 2009 to Citi Field, a 42,000-seat stadium. The new home borrows in appearance from the Brooklyn Dodgers' old Ebbets Field, with its grand Jackie Robinson Rotunda, and from the Polo Grounds, with its dark green seats.

Mets left fielder Endy Chavez robs the Cardinals' Scott Rolen of a home run in Game 7 of the 2006 NLCS. New York lost 3–1, however.

Citi Field is a nod to the city's proud NL heritage and a green canvas on which the Mets can paint their own colorful future.

The 2010 and 2011 seasons started out strong but ended in more disappointment.

More losing seasons plagued the team in 2012 and 2013. Still, there were highlights. In 2012, Santana pitched the first no-hitter in the team's history. That same year, Wright signed an eight-year contract. The Mets hope this star player will help bring home another World Series title.

TIMELINE

1961
The New York Metropolitan Baseball Club Inc. is accepted into the NL on March 6 and spends $1.8 million to draft 22 players on October 10.

1962
The Mets lose their first regular-season game 11–4 to the host St. Louis Cardinals on April 11. New York's first win, 9–1 over the Pirates in Pittsburgh, does not come until April 23. Jay Hook earns the victory.

1964
The first game at Shea Stadium is a 4–3 Mets loss to the Pirates on April 17.

1966
On April 2, the Mets win a lottery to draft Hall of Fame pitcher Tom Seaver.

1969
After finishing in ninth place the season before, the Mets clinch the NL East Division on September 24 with a 6–0 home win against the Cardinals. They go on to beat the Atlanta Braves in the NLCS and the Baltimore Orioles in the World Series.

1973
The Mets, who were in last place as late as August 30, clinch the NL East on October 1 and finish with an 82–79 record. They beat the Cincinnati Reds in the NLCS.

1980
A group headed by Nelson Doubleday and Fred Wilpon buys the Mets on January 24 for an estimated $21.1 million—then the highest amount paid for an American pro sports franchise. Doubleday is the great-great-grandnephew of Abner Doubleday, whom some credit with inventing baseball.

1986	The Mets win the pennant by outlasting the host Houston Astros 7–6 in 16 innings in Game 6 of the NLCS. The Mets rally at home in Game 6 and Game 7 of the World Series to defeat the Boston Red Sox.
1997	On June 16 at Yankee Stadium, Dave Mlicki pitches a 6–0 shutout in the Mets' first regular-season game ever against the New York Yankees.
1999	Todd Pratt's homer eliminates the Arizona Diamondbacks in the NLDS. Robin Ventura's walk-off, fence-clearing single beats the Braves in Game 5 of the NLCS. But the Braves prevail in the next game to win the series.
2000	Bobby Jones ousts the San Francisco Giants with a one-hitter in Game 4 of the NLDS. Mike Hampton knocks out the Cardinals with a three-hitter in Game 5 of the NLCS.
2006	The Mets complete a three-game sweep over the Dodgers in the NLDS with a 9–5 win in Los Angeles, then take the Cardinals to seven games in the NLCS before losing at home on a ninth-inning homer by Yadier Molina.
2007	The Mets miss the postseason despite leading the NL East by seven games with 17 remaining.
2008	The Mets miss the postseason again despite leading the division by 3 1/2 games with 17 left. The last game, a 4–2 loss to the Florida Marlins on September 28, is the final one ever at Shea.
2009	The Mets lose their Citi Field debut 6–5 to the San Diego Padres on April 13.
2012	Johan Santana pitches the first no-hitter in the Mets history. David Wright signs an eight-year contract with the Mets.

QUICK STATS

FRANCHISE HISTORY

1962–

WORLD SERIES
(wins in bold)

1969, 1973, **1986**, 2000

NL CHAMPIONSHIP SERIES
(1969–)

1969, 1973, 1986, 1988, 1999, 2000, 2006

DIVISION CHAMPIONSHIPS
(1969–)

1969, 1973, 1986, 1988, 2006

KEY PLAYERS
(position[s]; seasons with team)

Gary Carter (C; 1985–89)
John Franco (RP; 1990–2004)
Dwight Gooden (SP; 1984–94)
Keith Hernandez (1B; 1983–89)
Howard Johnson (3B/SS/OF;
    1985–93)
Cleon Jones (OF; 1963, 1965–75)
Jerry Koosman (SP; 1967–78)
Ed Kranepool (1B/OF; 1962–79)
Tug McGraw (RP; 1965–67, 1969–74)
Mike Piazza (C; 1998–2005)
Jose Reyes (SS; 2003–11)
Tom Seaver (SP; 1967–77, 1983)
Darryl Strawberry (OF; 1983–90)
David Wright (3B; 2004–)

KEY MANAGERS

Gil Hodges (1968–71):
    339–309; 7–1 (postseason)
Davey Johnson (1984–90):
    595–417; 11–9 (postseason)

HOME FIELDS

Polo Grounds (1962–63)
Shea Stadium (1964–2008)
Citi Field (2009–)

* All statistics through 2013 season

QUOTES AND ANECDOTES

Meet the Mets,
Meet the Mets,
Step right up and greet the Mets,
Bring your kiddies,
Bring your wife,
Guaranteed to have the time of your life . . .
—Part of the Mets' theme song, written by Ruth Roberts and Bill Katz

When the Mets' Jimmy Piersall hit his 100th career home run in 1963, he celebrated by backpedaling around the bases.

"Seven hundred defeats later, here we are."
—First baseman Ed Kranepool, before the start of the 1969 NLCS

Before the Mets' home game on April 22, 1970, against the San Diego Padres, Tom Seaver was honored for winning the 1969 Cy Young Award as the NL's best pitcher. That afternoon, he one-upped himself, tying a major league record with 19 strikeouts and breaking a major league mark by fanning the final 10 batters. "He was like a machine those last few innings," teammate and first baseman Ed Kranepool said. "Whomp. Whomp. Whomp."

On August 13, 2010, R. A. Dickey pitched the 27th complete-game one-hitter in Mets history as New York beat the visiting Philadelphia Phillies 1–0. In 2012, Johan Santana pitched the club's first no-hitter.

GLOSSARY

acquire

To add a player, usually through the draft, free agency, or a trade.

berth

A place, spot, or position, such as in the baseball playoffs.

commissioner

A person authorized to perform certain tasks or endowed with certain powers.

expansion

In sports, the addition of a franchise or franchises to a league.

exploits

Acts of brilliance.

franchise

An entire sports organization, including the players, coaches, and staff.

heroics

Important deeds successfully carried out in the face of danger.

metropolitan

Referring to a core city and its immediate surrounding areas.

miracle

An event that defies the laws of science and is thought to have supernatural causes.

pennant

A flag. In baseball, it symbolizes that a team has won its league championship.

platoon

A unit or group of people within a team.

stratosphere

A high level of Earth's atmosphere.

terrorists

People who use violence as a way to strike fear in others.

FOR MORE INFORMATION

Further Reading

Green, David. *101 Reasons to Love the Mets*. New York: Stewart, Tabori & Chang, 2008.

Lichtenstein, Michael. *Ya Gotta Believe: The 40th Anniversary New York Mets Fan Book*. New York: St. Martin's Griffin, 2002.

Silverman, Matthew. *100 Things Mets Fans Should Know & Do Before They Die*. Chicago: Triumph Books, 2008.

Websites

To learn more about Inside MLB, visit **booklinks.abdopublishing.com**. These links are routinely monitored and updated to provide the most current information available.

Places to Visit

Citi Field
123-01 Roosevelt Avenue
Flushing, NY 11368
718-507-6387
http://mlb.mlb.com/nym/ballpark/citifield_overview.js
This has been the Mets' home field since 2009. The team plays 81 regular-season games here each year. Tours are available when the Mets are not playing.

Mets Spring Training
Digital Domain Park
525 Northwest Peacock Boulevard
Port St. Lucie, FL 34986
772-871-2115
This has been the Mets' spring-training ballpark since 1988.

National Baseball Hall of Fame and Museum
25 Main Street
Cooperstown, NY 13326
888-HALL-OF-FAME
www.baseballhall.org
This hall of fame and museum highlights the greatest players and moments in the history of baseball. Tom Seaver and Gary Carter are among the former Mets enshrined here.

INDEX

About the Author

Andy Knobel has worked at the *Baltimore Sun* since 1988, most recently as the Sports Deputy Editor for Nights. He was raised on Long Island and in New York City during the Mets' formative years. He lives in Columbia, Maryland, with his wife and two children.